D0828229

Xtreme Athletes
David Beckham

David Beckham

Calvin Craig Miller

MORGAN REYNOLDS
PUBLISHING

Greensboro, North Carolina

Xtreme Athletes

Michael Phelps
David Beckham
Danica Patrick
Kelly Slater
Shaun White

XTREME ATHLETES: DAVID BECKHAM

Copyright © 2009 by Calvin Craig Miller

Library of Congress Cataloging-in-Publication Data

Miller, Calvin Craig, 1954-
  Xtreme athletes : David Beckham / by Calvin Craig Miller.
    p. cm.
  Includes bibliographical references and index.
  ISBN-13: 978-1-59935-082-0
  ISBN-10: 1-59935-082-3
  1. Beckham, David, 1975- 2. Soccer players--England--Biography. 3.
Celebrities--England--Biography. I. Title. II. Title: David Beckham.
  GV942.7.B432M54 2008
  796.334092--dc22
  [B]
                                        2007047792

Printed in the United States of America

First Edition

For Steven

Contents

David Beckham
(Courtesy of George Pimentel/WireImage)

one
Footballs for Christmas

David Beckham was a soccer fan long before he was a superstar. Born on May 2, 1975, the son of Ted and Sandra Beckham, he was raised in a working-class neighborhood in London, England. Soccer was a Beckham family tradition, one encouraged by his father Ted, an accomplished player himself.

David's Christmas presents always included items for his favorite sport, football. (In almost all countries except the United States, soccer is called football.) Every year, he got a new football and team uniforms. Presents from his father's parents and his own parents displayed a friendly rivalry between the two. His

Beckham's parents, Ted and Sandra *(Courtesy of ZUMA Press)*

father Ted was an avid Manchester United fan, his paternal grandfather equally committed to Arsenal.

Ted hated Arsenal but put up with a holiday ritual that must have tried his patience. David would get a Manchester United uniform from his parents and try it on. He would get the Arsenal kit from his grandparents and dutifully don it as well. With soccer so rooted in his family tree, it is little wonder he went onto a career as a pro.

David's family still has a video of him playing football just after Christmas one year, decked out in a Manchester United jersey. He was a little more than three years old.

Ted Beckham did not force David to play the game, nor to choose sides. But he watched every Manchester United game he could and was perhaps even more devoted to the game than the average English fan. What's more, Ted played the game himself with great skill and enthusiasm.

Manchester United Crash of 1958

Manchester United fans have never forgotten an air tragedy that occurred on February 6, 1958. The team boarded a flight back to England from a European Cup match against the Yugoslavian team Red Star Belgrade.

The plane landed in Munich, Germany for a refueling stop. When the aircraft took off

The plane crash that killed eight members of the 1958 Manchester United team *(Courtesy of AP Images)*

from the Munich airport, it hit a patch of slush, and slowed down below the speed required to get airborne. It failed to gain enough altitude to clear a fence surrounding the airport. The plane struck the fence, and then crashed into an unoccupied house.

Seven United players died at the scene. An eighth, Duncan Edwards, later died from injuries. Injuries forced the retirement of another two.

Many people thought the club would disband after the disaster. Instead, they fielded a team made up of youth players and reserves. At the first match following the crash, United won a 3-0 victory against Sheffield. The program for the game showed a blank space opposite the name of each crash victim. The team did not play well that season, but the tragedy only increased the loyalty of United fans, including David's father Ted.

Ted was on a semiprofessional team called Kingfisher. He threw everything he had into games and had only one fault that David remembers. His father was a hard charging player, frequently called for being offside, a rule that prevents players from being too near their opponents' goal line. David and his mom Sandra, along with his older sister Lynne and his younger sister Joanne, came along to cheer Dad on. Lynne didn't like the game at all. Joanne, who tagged along after David so much that he called her his "little mate," came to love football.

A young David shows his support for the England soccer team. *(Stuart Robinson/Express UK/ZUMA Press)*

Few young fans could match David's passion. He simply never saw himself doing anything but playing football for a living. He played in pick-up games with neighborhood kids. David's friends knew of his passion, and frequently his mother would answer the door to find a gaggle of young soccer players wanting to know if he could come out and play. When he was not playing a match, he might be found with a single friend playing "keepy-uppy," a game in which players attempt to keep a ball airborne with any part of the body allowed in soccer, which excludes the arms.

At Chingford Primary, the first school he attended, he neglected his studies and even today remembers little of the subjects his instructors attempted to teach. The only thing he applied himself to was his art classes. He loved to draw the characters of Disney comic books and even drew his own made-up characters.

Other subjects bored him as well. He realized in time that he missed much by paying too little attention to his schoolwork.

As a boy, David told everyone he would play for Manchester United. It might have seemed a far-fetched notion at the time. Most of the boys with whom he played the game went on to make their careers in other fields. But David's dreams left no room for thoughts of any other future. His father's ambitions also became wrapped in the dream of soccer fame for his only son.

Some of David's fondest memories spring from the days he would accompany his dad to the Wadham Lodge club where his father played and practiced for the Kingfisher team. He envied the well-laid out grounds, regulation nets, and the several fields, including one for the important cup games, kept by his father's team.

When the field had emptied, his father would watch as David practiced free kicks, the kind of kicks awarded players when the other team commits a foul. Good kicks got an extra fifty pence added to his allowance.

It was at the Kingfisher practices David first competed with players considerably bigger than him. He was a skinny kid who could gain no weight no matter how much he ate. Yet when his father's teammates neared the end of practice, they would sometimes let him play on a five-man squad. On a rare occasion, his father objected to an overly aggressive tackle against David by one of the adult players. Mostly, though, he let his son mix it up with the others. Both of them thought his playing against adults helped his game. David considered the invitation to play a great compliment.

"I was so excited to be out there playing with the rest of them—these grown men—that I took whatever I had coming," he wrote later.

Not all of his friends shared his passion. One of his best friends was his neighbor John Brown. John could sometimes be persuaded to play a little, but he mostly preferred indoor games. He liked Lego and Gameboy, and David would play to keep his friend happy. Sandra would drop her son and his friends off at neighborhood movie theaters. Other times they would take a short cut to a park nearby where they would drink soft drinks and eat chocolate. He defied his mother's rule against riding skateboards by using friends' boards. He once had to hide his scrapped legs after he took a spill.

The first school he attended offered him the chance to play on a strong soccer team. Mr. McGhee, a teacher at Chase Lane Primary, was the coach. Mr. McGhee was Scottish, an enthusiastic fan of the sport, and a tough man on his team. When he was angry about players' mistakes, he would throw temper

David playing soccer in 1986 *(Courtesy of Stuart Robinson/Express UK/ ZUMA Press)*

tantrums, hurling teacups and balls against walls. David was so eager to play, he was happy to accept any team or coach. He later joined the Roger Morgan Soccer School, run by a former player for the Spurs professional team, one of the first of several such schools he attended while growing up.

He got his first taste of international competition when he joined the Ridgeway Rovers, a boys' team set up by a stocky coach named Stuart Underwood. Underwood arranged matches with boys' teams in Holland and Germany. His dad became a coach for Ridgeway. Coach Underwood kept tight rules. He required the boys to show up for big games wearing collars and ties. Missing a practice meant forfeiting one's chance to play in weekend games. It was with the Rovers that David suffered his first sports injury. He began to experience pains in his heels that grew steadily worse. Eventually he had to sit out for five weeks. "That was the longest five weeks of my life and, in a way, I've never gotten over it," he wrote.

He rejoined the team and played with more passion than ever. During the three years he played for the Ridgeway Rovers, he scored more than one hundred goals.

Between the years he was ten and eleven, David went through a trial that prepared him for the ups and downs of a life in sports. He entered the Bobby Charlton Skills Tournament in 1986, traveling to the city of Manchester in central England. The tournament held special significance for Manchester United fans, since it was named for a former player. But David entered the contest with a toothache and did not play well enough to win. The pain of losing hurt worse than the tooth.

He made a comeback in the same tournament the next year. On the field of Old Trafford, where his Manchester United heroes played their games, David won the skills competition. Charlton himself presented him with the trophy.

Older members of the Beckham family helped David nurture his talents. His mother did a balancing act between her job as a hairdresser, driving a minibus to practices, and trying to make sure the family at least got together for a hot dinner. His older sister looked out for him at school. When he got beaten up in a fight once, she told the teachers what had happened and drove him home. But Lynne never came to love the game as she did her brother.

The roles were reversed with David and Joanne.

His younger sister loved to tag along with him. She became a football fan because her brother was a player. She learned to tend goal so he could practice in the backyard.

His relationship with Joanne led him to take over some of the baby-sitting chores from his mother while she was cooking or working. It was about this time that David also began taking on roles traditionally associated with females. He began serving tea and biscuits for his mother's clients when she did their hair at home. He took Home Economics in secondary school to get out of science and discovered a flair for cooking. The press would later chide him for not living up to the macho image of a football player, but David was never concerned about meeting their expectations, only his own.

His parents discovered the most effective way to discipline him was to make him sit out a practice for breaking their rules. "That killed me," he wrote. "It was the worst punishment I could ever have had." He made his share of mistakes growing up, but learned to do whatever it took to avoid this harsh penalty.

He played on his school team at Chingford High, along with his district and county teams. The county team of Essex took David on his longest trip yet, when it traveled to Texas. He fell in love with the United States. The Americans took good care of the players, and the son of the family that hosted David played for one of the tournament teams.

Just as soccer provided David with a ticket to see a world beyond his East London neighborhood, it also taught him discipline he might otherwise have lacked. Some of his friends began smoking or drinking on Saturday nights. David did not join them. Saturday was the night before the Sunday match. He spent his evenings inside watching soccer clips on television and went to bed early.

His dedication brought its rewards. Professional scouts had begun to watch his performance with the Ridgeway Rovers. He joined the North London youth team of the Tottenham Hotspurs, also known as the Spurs. His grandfather on his mother's side was an avid Spurs fan, forming yet another fork of the game in the Beckham family tree. Pleasing his grandfather pleased David, but he still wanted nothing more than to play for Man United.

One day after a game with his district club, he went back to the car park to find his mother with tears in her eyes. She told him he was lucky he had played a good game, and he asked why. She pointed to a stranger. "That man over there: he's a Man United scout," she said. "They want to have a look at you." They both broke out in tears. While his mother probably had mixed emotions, David wept only from joy.

two

The Fledgling Footballer

The Manchester United scout's name was Malcolm Fidgeon. He came to the Beckhams' house and talked to David and his parents about his soccer skills and the boy's future in the game. Before committing, the club wanted to give David a tryout with its youth team. Fidgeon and David became friends, as the scout drove his young prospect back and forth from London to Manchester.

The tryouts helped David get his foot on the first rung of the professional soccer ladder. England's soccer teams use a three-step system for moving players into the pro ranks. After the youth team, a player may be called to serve on the reserve team. If and when they are good enough, players finally may graduate to the first team.

Just getting in the door was exhilarating for this boy who had centered his life around football. At the club's Manchester facilities, everyone focused on the sport all day. When they weren't kicking the ball, they were talking about soccer.

Team officials liked what they saw in David. One night at home, his father answered the phone. The caller turned out to be Alex Ferguson, manager of Manchester United. Ted Beckham looked stunned when he announced the news.

"He said you're just the kind of boy Manchester United is looking for," Ted told his son.

The great news might have settled David's plans quickly, but the young player found himself involved in a bidding war between two clubs. The Tottenham Hotspurs, or Spurs, also decided they wanted David Beckham. The boy had grown up dreaming of playing for United, but still, it was no snap decision. The Spurs were his maternal grandfather's favorite team, and they played in London, which would have made it easier for his family and friends to attend games.

He might have chosen Man United in any event, but his meeting with the two managers tilted his decision. When a Spurs official ushered David into the office of Spurs manager Terry Venables, they found Venables looking on the floor for something he'd dropped. During the interview, Venables came off as knowing little about David's skills. By contrast, Ferguson knew almost everything there was to know about the young player and treated him like royalty. While he and his parents were still weighing his decision, the Manchester United staff even baked a cake for David's thirteenth birthday on May 2, 1988.

The clubs made very similar offers, lucrative six-year contracts. David made the decision to sign with United. He later admitted he would have probably gone with his childhood heroes in any event.

Eric Harrison coached the youth division of United. He was a man who combined great affection for his players with a no-nonsense work ethic. He loved molding young men into the best players they could be, but would not hesitate to take them down a peg if they played poorly. To this day, David counts Harrison as one of his most influential coaches. He praised David for playing well. He also chewed him out, for such errors as making passes that were more flashy than effective.

"What are you playing at? Hitting those flippin' Hollywood passes all day?" he demanded.

David playing for the
Manchester United youth
team *(Courtesy of Shaun
Botterill/Allsport)*

Harrison's players of the late 1980s and early 1990s achieved a rare distinction in being compared to a legendary group of 1950s players. During that era, Manchester United manager Matt Busby nurtured a future group of superstars dubbed Busby's Babes. After they proved they could win, Harrison's group became "Fergie's Fledglings," a future crop of potential stars for Ferguson. They included Gary and Phil Neville, Nicky Butt, and Ryan Giggs, all of whom went on to successful careers.

While gradually making a name for himself, David dealt with pressures similar to those any teenager might face away from home. He stayed with a series of landlords arranged by the team. One of the first was a Scottish couple whom David really liked at first. But the husband angered David and his dad, when he cuffed the teen in the ear for losing his key. He finally ended up in a room right across from the stadium, which he loved because it allowed him to sleep longer before getting up to practice. He brought a stereo from home and bought a television. He met a Manchester girl named Deana who became his girlfriend for several years.

Fergie's Fledglings proved their talent when they won the Football Association (FA) Youth Cup in 1992. United defeated the Spurs to advance to the championship round against Crystal Palace. David scored one goal in a 3-1 victory in the first match. United earned the championship with 3-2 triumph in the second. Bobby Charlton, one of the Busby Babes, said they were the best of any English club he had ever seen.

David's dad warned him not to take his youth team successes as a premature sign of accomplishment. David could only prove himself when he got to the first team and achieved at the highest level. David did not think he really needed that advice. He hadn't dreamed his whole life of being a contributor on a youth squad.

Soon after the Youth Cup win, Ferguson decided to test his would-be stars. He promoted David, along with several others, for a match in the League Cup. The League Cup is a relatively low-level event, which is why he considered it a good proving ground. David could not help feeling some pride, however. He was only seventeen when he got his first minutes on the first team.

He got off to a rough start. Ferguson called him in late in the game. David went in and played what he considered decent football. After the game, though, Ferguson chewed him out for a lackluster performance. David realized much more would be expected of him at the top professional level.

David charges after the ball during a premiership match against Chelsea.
(Courtesy of Gary M. Prior/Allsport)

Beyond the League Cup, the top three competitions of club play are the English Premier League, the Football Association Cup, and the Champions League, an international event. In 1994-1995, David played again in League Cup matches. He got another step up when Ferguson put him in against a Turkish team in the Champions League, after United had been eliminated. David made a personal milestone by kicking in his first goal at the first-team level. Ferguson made no mention of it after the game.

It was all part of the transition from an outstanding young player to professional. Ferguson may have been letting the young players know that extremely high caliber play was to be expected from players on England's top pro rosters. Still, David began to feel a sense of insecurity about his future.

Early in 1995, the team gave him news that he considered quite threatening. He was being sent down to Preston North End, a small club. David had been around soccer long enough to know small club demotions could mark the end of a player's career.

three

Winning with Kids

Alex Ferguson did not send David to the small Preston North End club with the notion of scrubbing him from Manchester United. He only wanted to give him some experience at a different level. Before David departed for his new assignment, the manager called him in and assured him he still had a place on the team.

He was glad to hear it. He drove to his first day of training in a Ford Escort, but his modest vehicle did not dispel the belief of some lower division players that David Beckham considered himself big time. He suspected they considered him a "right flash sod," a big shot. He did not improve his standing with his teammates after his first practice when he tossed his

Alex Ferguson *(Courtesy of AP Images/Phil Noble/PA)*

dirty uniform on the floor. No one cleans uniforms for lower-division players as they do for top-tier teams like Manchester United. Beckham was informed he was to wash his own uniform and have it ready by the next day.

Preston North End players gained respect for David as he made it clear he did not consider himself above them. He attended community events with the team, and more importantly, scored for them in games. He was sad to leave when he was called back up after five games.

The sadness disappeared the following week, when Ferguson called him in for his first start. This marked another milestone, the time when Ted Beckham had told his son that he could begin to count his professional accomplishments. He ran onto the home field in front of 40,000 fans for a match with Leeds United. He was nineteen years old.

Beckham got his first start in part because he was a midfielder, a position Ferguson was short on in the Leeds United match. Midfielders play between the forwards (those who play closest to the opponents' goal) and fullbacks (defenders who play close to their own goal). Midfielders run more than other positions and so must have a great deal of stamina.

His first full year as a starter came with the 1995-96 season, a year when Ferguson used a lot of his younger players. Beckham scored in his first game, but United lost. Harsh criticism quickly followed.

Beckham found himself part of a controversy in the sports media. On the television show *Match of the Day*, commentator Alan Hansen sniped "you can't win anything with kids."

Alex Ferguson came under pressure because the team had played poorly the previous season and had ended up with no major trophies. Soccer in England does not have playoffs, such as those in American football. Each team in the English Premier League (EPL) plays an away and home game against every other team. The team with the most points wins the EPL championship.

Teams also compete for the Football Association Cup. A random drawing is held to determine opponents

How football began

Games similar to football can be found in cultures throughout recorded history. The Chinese played games involving a kicked ball 3000 years ago. The Greeks, Romans, and Persians also played such games, although rules and customs regarding play varied from one civilization to another. Football games were often part of military drills.

Modern football began in the mid-1800s in England, when boys' schools competed in a variety of ball games at least vaguely resembling today's sport. But rules varied widely, with disagreement on how rough the game should be and whether contact should be allowed with the arms.

In October of 1863, representatives of the schools decided to settle the conflicting rules. They formed and met in Freemason's Tavern in London, thus marking the beginning of England's Football Association (FA).

The members argued and divided themselves into two camps. Some wanted to establish rules that allowed considerable roughness and use of the hands. The prevailing majority, however, wanted penalties for those actions. Those who disagreed split off and formed a league for rugby, a sport more similar to football played in the United States.

The FA Cup pitting English teams against one another was first played in 1872. The game grew in popularity in the late 1800s, spreading throughout Europe. In 1904, the Fédération Internationale de Football Association (FIFA) was formed in Paris. Today teams in more than two hundred countries play the game. It is the world's most popular spectator sport.

in any given match. Clubs of lower divisions are included, so a major team like Manchester United could play a minor club. Losers are eliminated until only two teams survive to play in the finals. The crowning achievement is the Champions League, where teams throughout England and Europe compete against one another. Winning two of these championships is called doing the Double. Earning three of them is the Treble.

With all these trophies to be claimed, a manager is under considerable pressure to snag at least one. It's little wonder that Ferguson chewed his players out when they failed to perform well, for the English media rode him just as hard when United failed.

Fergie's Fledglings helped redeem Ferguson's reputation in Beckham's first year as a starter.

After dropping their first game, they reeled off a five-match win streak. In the chase for the FA Cup, Newcastle proved the foe to beat. At one point, Newcastle held a fourteen-point lead over Manchester United. Eric Cantona, a high-scoring but hot-tempered player who had been suspended for kicking a fan, gave a strong boost to the team when he returned in October. Cantona helped spark a run which overtook Newcastle, as Man United proceeded into the semifinals of the FA Cup. In the match against The Blues of Chelsea, Beckham enjoyed one of his brightest moments when he booted in the game winner.

In the EPL race running at the same time, Manchester United took a lead over Newcastle. The climax came in the title-clinching match versus Middlesbrough. United won the game 3-0 and took the EPL title. Now Beckham and all the other Man United players turned their sights to the final of the FA Cup. Their opponent was to be archrival club Liverpool.

The FA Cup holds an especially revered place in the hearts of English soccer fans. At one time, it was the only televised match of the season. (The owners of the teams feared televised games would hurt ticket sales.) Established in 1871, it is the world's

Beckham celebrates after scoring a goal. *(Courtesy of Shaun Botterill/Allsport UK)*

oldest soccer championship. "Every schoolboy's dream is about playing in the Cup Final," Beckham wrote later.

It was a brilliantly sunny day at Wembley Stadium in London when United took the field against Liverpool. Playing on a sticky field where the grass had been left long, both teams struggled to find the goal. The game remained scoreless until late in the second half. With a minute left to play, Beckham tried a corner kick. Liverpool goalkeeper David James got a hand

Beckham and teammate Gary Neville hold the FA Cup during a celebration parade in 1996. *(Courtesy of John Peters/Manchester United/Getty Images)*

on the ball to keep it out, but Cantona volleyed it back in.

The team carried Cantona off the field. Manager Alex Ferguson might have talked to his team after most games but not that day. United players raised a raucous din, shouting, singing, and spraying one another with champagne. The best of Fergie's Fledglings had won their first professional medals. The team that had been warned it would win nothing by playing kids like Beckham had done the Double.

four

Bending the Long Shot

After Manchester United won the Double in 1996, Beckham decided to get away from soccer for a while. He spent his vacation in Sardinia, an Italian island in the Mediterranean Sea. He loafed in the sun, enjoying swimming, walks on the beach, and pasta dinners.

His brief rest from the game did nothing to diminish his skills. He proved as much in the first game of the next season, when he made one of the spectacular plays that has made him a legend of football.

United played Wimbledon in the season opener. Beckham took some ribbing from the other players before the game started. His sponsor, adidas, had sent him a pair of shoes but the name was wrong. He was walking around with "Charlie" on the tongue of his boots, for Charlie Miller, a player for the Glasgow Rangers. He was the joke of the dressing room for only a short while, though. There would be no jokes about his shoes by the time the game ended.

David Beckham's moment came in the final minute, with Man United up 2-0. Brian McClair made a pass to Beckham at midfield. A player would usually hold or pass the ball, but Beckham had noticed Wimbledon goalkeeper Neil Sullivan playing a long way out of goal. He decided to just take the shot.

Manager Alex Ferguson thought Beckham had lost his mind. But the goal caught Sullivan unawares and sailed into the net. Fans rose to their feet and the stadium erupted in a roar. Afterwards, a reporter from *Match of the Day* wanted to interview Beckham by phone, but Ferguson would not allow it. Spectacular shot or not, he wanted his players to remain focused on the bigger picture, of winning championships.

But no player could boot a goal from midfield without creating a sensation. Everywhere Beckham went people were talking about it. He called his girlfriend at her college. She had not seen the game and was puzzled about what had happened. Fans were singing his praises all over the campus, and

Beckham celebrates at the match against Wimbledon in 1997, during which he scored a long-range goal that catapulted him to fame. *(Courtesy of Mike Cooper/Allsport UK)*

all she knew was that everyone considered David Beckham's midfield goal some kind of miracle.

To this day, he keeps a photo of the goal at home. "When my foot struck that ball, it kicked open the door to the rest of my life at the same time. . . . In the life of David Beckham, it feels like the ball is still up there," he wrote.

Manchester United players have many fans. They sign autographs and give interviews to newspapers and television. But Beckham was no longer just one of the United players. He had become a star. The role was one that would bring him benefits as well as the burden of being constantly in the public eye.

His star power soon increased dramatically because of a new love interest. He later remembered a kind of rare love at first sight when he was watching the pop music group the Spice Girls in a hotel room the night prior to a game in 1996.

The group was extremely popular, and he had seen them before. He had even picked out his favorite member, Victoria Adams, also known as Posh Spice. He was watching the television with friend and teammate Gary Neville, and Beckham began talking obsessively about Adams. He told Neville that he intended to try and meet her. He had no clear plan for doing so, however. The Spice Girls' records were

Victoria Adams (second from right) with the Spice Girls *(Courtesy of AP Images/Remy de la Mauviniere)*

at the top of the charts. Man United fans might be impressed with Beckham, but it was no guarantee that Adams would be.

It turned out the gulf between them was not so great as it might have first appeared. Adams had grown up in Goff's Oak, a short drive from

Beckham's London neighborhood of Chingford. Beckham didn't even know her last name, though, when his long distance crush on her first bloomed.

Meeting her turned out to be easier than he had ever imagined. A month or so later, Adams and fellow Spice Girl Melanie Chisholm, showed up at a United game in London. He found the two sipping wine in the players' lounge. He didn't even have to introduce himself. Their manager, Simon Fuller, came to Beckham and offered to make the introductions.

After all of his obsessing over Adams, Beckham's shyness overcame him in their first meeting. He found he could say little more than hello. They spoke only briefly before Adams rejoined Chisholm. Beckham got back on the team bus without even having gotten her number. He cursed himself.

What Beckham did not know was that Adams had her eye on him as well. Before showing up in the players lounge, she had been doing a photo shoot in which the Spice Girls had dressed in soccer team uniforms. She had seen his picture in an album and had decided to wear a United uniform. She did not know anything about soccer but thought Beckham quite handsome.

She showed up again at the Old Trafford football grounds for a United home game. Again he met her in the team lounge, and this time, managed to hold himself together long enough to really talk to her. They soon forgot about others in the room. He was so focused on the attractive pop star that he was surprised to find the lounge nearly empty when he looked up. They had lost track of time.

She asked him for his number. Fearing she might not call, he insisted on taking hers instead. For their first date, they went to a Chinese restaurant. They did not feel much like eating, and when they had sat there for a while drinking Cokes without ordering anything, the owner threw them out. She had no idea who either of them was.

They soon had gone past flirting and settled into a committed relationship. When the next season started, Beckham's thoughts were split between his football and his new glamorous girlfriend. They talked for hours on their cell phones, even when she had to travel halfway around the world for concerts. He ordered roses for her every time she arrived at a new hotel.

His obsession with Adams had little effect on his game. He was tapped for the English national team in 1996, a distinction that allowed him the honor of

Beckham stands with Victoria Adams in 1997. *(Courtesy of AP Images/John Giles)*

competing for the World Cup. He played his first time for England in September of 1996. Manchester United again won the league cup, and Beckham was voted the Professional Footballers' Association Young Player of the Year in 1997. He felt on top of the world. He had no idea that the next year his soaring fame would turn to national disgrace, as one disastrous mistake would cast a shadow over all his accomplishments.

five

Disgrace and Redemption

N o one could have predicted disaster when David Beckham took the field for England's national match against Argentina in the 1998 World Cup. The twenty-three-year-old midfielder had seemed destined for greatness in the game of soccer.

He had played superbly for his home team of Manchester United, scoring to help win the Football Association Youth Cup in 1992, only a year after he was signed. In the 1996-97 season, he had scored one of the most famous goals of modern times, when he fired a ball into the net from more than fifty yards away in a United game against Wimbledon. He had been voted Young Player of the Year. Even in the current competition, which would bring about one of the worst episodes in his career, he had scored on a spectacular free kick in an early round against Columbia, and was proclaimed a national hero.

There seemed to be no stopping this fiercely attacking young fireball, with his pin point passes and his deadly eye for the goal. He was always eager to take the field, and never more so than in England's World Cup match against its bitter rival Argentina in Saint-Etienne, France.

The game got off to a bad start for England. English player David Seaman drew a foul, and Argentina took the opportunity to score. Alan Shearer came back to tie the game for England. Michael Owen made a great goal for England when he kicked the ball in from fourteen yards out. Argentina scored again to tie the game at half time.

Beckham's trouble came two minutes into the second half, in a fateful confrontation with Diego Simeone. The Argentinean player was an expert in taunting opponents, forcing them to commit costly penalties. Simeone ran into Beckham, then touched his head while he was still on the ground, as though to ruffle his hair. Beckham then committed the gravest error for a soccer player, kicking back at Simeone in retaliation. The official handed out the

Beckham receives a red card after retaliating against Diego Simeone during a 1998 World Cup match. *(Courtesy of AP Images/Denis Doyle)*

ultimate penalty: a red card ejecting him from the match. Argentina went on to win 4-3 in overtime.

Anyone could have seen it was bad play on Beckham's part. But anyone not familiar with the

Football rules

The international rules of soccer, called football in most countries, are simple in most cases. As usual in games with balls, the object is to make more goals than the opposing team.

Players kick a ball shaped like a sphere, which can vary between twenty-seven and twenty-eight inches in circumference. Players score goals when they kick or "head" (strike the ball with the head) so that the ball passes through the goal posts beneath the crossbar.

The field is marked with end lines at the goals, touchlines at the sides, a halfway line at midfield, and rectangular penalty and goal areas. The goals stand at opposite ends of the field. Two goals posts stand eight yards apart, connected by a crossbar, with a net behind. The goaltender must protect this area.

Eleven players are on each of the two teams. The referee makes the calls, with assistance from two linesmen. The game starts with a place kick from the center of the field. The kicking player, usually on the team which wins a coin toss, will try to kick the ball to a teammate.

No player other than the goalkeeper may touch the ball with their hands during on-field play. If the ball goes out of bounds, a player may throw it back in. The goalkeeper may throw or kick the ball to a teammate when it enters the penalty area.

A player may "dribble" the ball by controlling it with his or her feet while running downfield. Players may also pass the ball to another player. (Good passes are considered a crucial skill of the game, one at which David Beckham excels.) A player may not trip, push, or hold an opponent. An infraction of the rules will result in the opposing team being awarded a free kick. A direct kick may be kicked directly into the goal, whereas an indirect kick must first be touched by another player. The kind of infraction determines which kind of kick is given.

The most complicated rule is the offside infraction, one which frequently frustrated David's father, Ted, during his playing days. If an offensive player is nearer the goal line than the ball at the moment his teammate passes to him, he or she is offside, unless there are two defenders from the opposing team between the offensive player and the goal line. Various conditions can negate an offside call, such as when the offensive player receives the ball after it has been touched by a defensive player. The player must be participating in the play to be called offside.

A very serious infraction by a player will cause the referee to hand out a red card. One example is the kick Beckham gave to Argentina player Diego Simone in the 1998 World Cup. If a player receives a red card, the offender must leave the game and the team must continue to play with only ten players. This is why so many English fans blamed Beckham for the loss to Argentina.

fanaticism of some English soccer fans would have found the angry aftermath of the game beyond belief.

He tried at first to make amends through the press. "I have apologised to the England players and management and I want every England supporter to know how deeply sorry I am," he told reporters. But the press would prove one of his worst enemies in the coming controversy.

English manager Glenn Hoddle did not help Beckham in his own comments to the media. "David Beckham's sending off cost us dearly," Hoddle said. "I am not denying it cost us the game."

For months, Beckham was dogged by critical reporters and angry fans everywhere he turned. Public appearances put him at physical risk, as photographers and newspaper people surrounded him, demanding he answer such questions as whether he ought to leave the country. They once surrounded his car and fought with him as he tried to shut the doors. At some matches, fans gathered in the parking lots as though they were lynch mobs, shouting obscenities and threats as he passed. One newspaper printed a dart board with his face on it. Another summed up much of the nasty mood with the headline referring to the eleven-man English

World Cup squad: "TEN HEROIC LIONS, ONE STUPID BOY."

David saved all the stories about his disgrace in his scrapbook, the same one he kept for his good games and clippings about his honors. He knew if he could just keep playing, he would redeem himself. His great talent would prove him right.

After getting the red card, Beckham still had to get ready for another season with United. His job had been glamorous and exciting, but it was still a job. Now the hostile fans made it quite a grind.

Adams had told Beckham she was pregnant just before the ill-fated World Cup match. He had come to understand there were more important things than soccer in the world, but some of the fans did not agree. They refused to let go of their anger.

His friends and football colleagues tried to ease the pressure. His teammates, aware of the stress of crucial matches, were far less hard on him than the press. United manager Alex Ferguson told him not to worry about the slurs and insults, and insisted the fans at Manchester United were still behind him.

Practicing with his teammates kept him focused and for the most part kept distractions out of mind. But sometimes the controversy intruded on his life despite his best efforts. He could not help looking at the headlines, despite knowing they would have nothing good to say about him. On some occasions, the bad encounters came in face-to-face confrontations with grudge-holding fans. One day he and a teammate walked into a restaurant in Manchester for lunch. They had been there before, and liked the place because fans would let them eat in peace. Not this day though. It seemed almost as though everyone in the restaurant had turned to stare. Some of the people there looked as thought they wanted to kill Beckham. The two footballers ate their meals and left quickly.

Beckham knew he had to help United to a successful season. Otherwise, his name would become identified with his single worst mistake. His dad had already told him he should consider playing for a foreign team.

At the first home game, fans seemed to have erased the memory of the red card. As Man United played Leiceister City, most of the 60,000 at Old Trafford cheered him on. It was as though they knew he was getting blamed far beyond his due. He scored to tie the game, and the fans showed their appreciation. Beckham knew he would get far rougher treatment, though, once the team had to travel to an away game. More than anything, he just wanted to get one away game behind him, so he could put the insanity in perspective.

The match at Upton Park was everything Beckham had feared. A huge policeman arrived to escort him off the bus. Hundreds of angry people waited for him in the parking lot, having turned out to show their displeasure. They shouted filthy obscenities at him, despite the presence of their own children in some cases. Beckham had devoted his life to soccer, yet he could hardly believe anyone would let a game fill them with such rage.

No English team had ever won all three major crowns, but United found itself in the chase for the Premiership, the FA Cup, and the Champions League. Beckham faced an emotional game when his team played Internazionale of Italy, Diego Simeone's club team. He tried to make amends with the Argentinean who had needled him into the mistake of his career. The red card was still enough of a controversy that newspapers speculated about whether the two would shake hands. They did, and even exchanged jerseys at game's end.

Beckham felt the meeting with his nemesis had brought some closure to the event, although it would be years before he could completely put it out of his mind. The day after the match with Internazionale,

Beckham shakes hands with Diego Simeone as they exchange jerseys. *(Courtesy of Ben Radford/Allsport)*

he felt good. He was eating a candy bar when Adams called him with the news that the doctors had advised her to go into the hospital that night. The baby was on the way.

He raced to meet her at her parents' house, then drove her to the hospital. Beckham was the first to hold their new son, whom they named Brooklyn. Holding

Beckham with his son, Brooklyn *(Courtesy of AP Images/Phil Noble/PA)*

his baby was one of the greatest moments in his life, an experience to put soccer in perspective.

Soccer was still his job though, and the season was emerging as one with fantastic possibilities. No English team had ever won all three trophies required to do the Treble. But as Manchester United kept winning, it became apparent that this team could win the English Premiere League (EPL), the FA Cup, and the Champions League.

The main rival they had to get past was Arsenal. By April, United held a slight lead over Arsenal in points

Beckham in action during a 1999 FA Cup match against Arsenal *(Courtesy of Clive Brunskill /Allsport)*

for the EPL. The two faced each other in the semifinals of the FA Cup, played a scoreless tie, and had to play again. Beckham scored early, then Arsenal's Dennis Bergkamp tied the game. When United took a penalty late in the game, it looked as though Arsenal had the game in hand. Bergkamp was to get a penalty kick, and he almost never missed. But United goaltender Peter Schmeichel made a spectacular save that kept United alive for the thirty-minute overtime. Ryan Giggs kicked the winning goal for United at about the twenty-minute mark. As the game ended, fans went wild. They ran onto the field and began hoisting players, Beckham among them, for a victory ride on their shoulders. He had to remind fans to drop him near the dressing room.

United's advance toward a Champions League win was again slowed by a tie, when they played Juventus of Turin, Italy in a match where neither team scored. In the second match, United's Andy Cole broke a 2-2 tie with his game winner, and United was off to the finals.

The first match of the English Premiere League came against the team that had once courted Beckham before he signed with United, the Tottenham Spurs. The Spurs scored first but Beckham tied the game just before the half. Cole kicked in the game winner in the second half, and United had the first link of the Treble in hand.

By comparison, United's victory in the FA Cup championship was a walk in the park. United coasted to an easy 2-0 win over Newcastle and gained the second crown in the Treble. The players' celebration was muted. They all wanted the historic win by this point, and it would be anything but easy to capture a victory against Germany's Bayern Munich.

In the Champions League final, United staged one of the most dramatic comebacks in the history of the competition. The Germans took the field and settled down quickly, scoring just six minutes into the game. United goaltender Peter Schmeichel had his hands full, as he made one save after another to keep United in the game. But United could not find a way to get the ball in the goal. The referee signaled that only three minutes of injury time (time added to the match to compensate for time lost due to injuries) were left. Bayern ribbons were being tied around the trophy cup as United struggled for its life.

Then Teddy Sheringham sparked the comeback, when he booted a miskicked shot past Bayern goaltender Oliver Kahn. Beckham was near tears with relief, for it seemed United had snatched an overtime. Even more incredibly, they did not need

Ole Gunnar Solskjaer scores the winning goal for United to beat Bayern in the Champions League final. *(Courtesy of Allsport)*

the extra time. Beckham kicked the ball toward the near post, Sheringham sent the ball to Ole Gunnar Solskjaer, and Solskjaer kicked it in for the win. United fans erupted in cheers so loud it almost disrupted sportscasters attempt to call the game over.

One commentator summed up the mood when he proclaimed, "Manchester United have reached the promised land." United had indeed reached a new state of sports glory, and Beckham's bad night against Argentina suddenly seemed a long time ago.

six

Posh and Becks

The celebration after United's win over Munich went on for hours. Players were shouting and laughing in the dressing room, spraying each other with champagne. It took a lot longer than usual to clear the room, because everyone just wanted to savor the moment. Beckham was no exception. He took hold of the trophy and got the club photographer to take a picture of him with it. He found his dad and hugged him, thinking how sweet the triumph felt after all the bitterness of the past year.

Beckham went out to the football grounds and looked up at the empty stands. It amazed him to

Beckham poses with the trophy in the dressing room after United's win over Munich. *(Courtesy of John Peters/Manchester United/Getty Images)* think that less than an hour before, United's hopes of winning the game had looked so bleak.

The team's victory celebration in Manchester was a huge party with home fans, delirious with joy at Man United's success. A bus drove the team through the streets, packed with cheering fans at midday. It took hours for the bus to complete its route through the densely packed roads.

After the season, Beckham took some time to let the stress fade away. He clipped the newspaper stories of the team's victory, and put them in his scrapbook. It was a book that was surprisingly complete, including the scathing headlines and even the dartboard the newspaper had printed with his face on it. He wanted his record of his career to include the bad with the good.

He and Adams were married in July of 1999. The ceremony took a show business aura, as the footballer and the pop star became a phenomenon greater than either of them taken singly. They were "Posh and Becks" to the media, a couple who could not take a walk down the street without making headlines. Their wedding was a storybook affair held at a castle in Ireland. Manchester United teammate Gary Neville served as Beckham's best man. The magazine *OK!* bought the photo rights, which were such a rich prize that other publications tried to sneak photographers in.

The ceremony had much of the feel of a royal wedding. The couple sat in thrones, wearing crowns, and Brooklyn wore a purple suit. The baby brought Beckham back to Earth, when he threw up on both of them. Beckham was amused that his son had tarnished the fairy tale tone of the event. The wedding ended with a massive display of fireworks.

He and Adams wanted a house where they could raise Brooklyn and have enough room to let their family grow. They found a house in Hertfordshire, just north of London. Naturally enough, the English press came up with another snappy nickname for the Beckford home, calling it "Beckingham Palace," after the royal family's residence, Buckingham Palace.

Meanwhile, Beckham was beginning to have frequent quarrels with Alex Ferguson, the United manager who had brought him on and had once spoken so glowingly of his career. Ferguson had begun to suspect Beckham thought himself larger than the team, and the "Posh and Becks" treatment from the press only added to his suspicion. When Beckham sought a couple of days extra vacation so he could take a long honeymoon with Adams, Ferguson chewed him out. Beckham took it as a sign

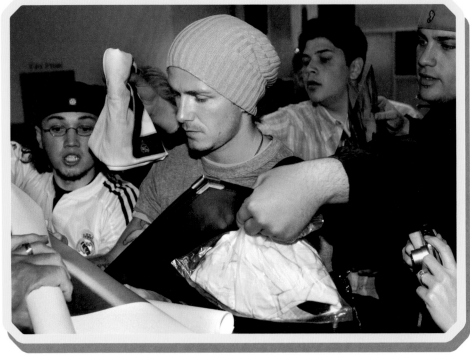

Fans hound Beckham for autographs. *(Courtesy of AP Images/Adam Rountree)*

that the manager wanted to make sure he did not let his ego get away with him after the Treble wins and the star treatment he was now getting from the press. Still, he felt the manager was being unreasonable, a feeling that would grow more intense over the next few seasons.

Manchester United showed much of the excellent form it had in the previous season, as it cruised to an easy victory in the Premiership. Beckham earned some personal glory by way of several second place best-player finishes, being named second best player for both Europe and the world. He also earned runner-up for BBC Sports Personality of the Year.

What he did on the field had fallen to secondary importance in the eyes of those who were more fans of Posh and Becks than they were of soccer. He learned that some while some people follow stars because they love them, others do so for the opposite reason. He was surprised one day when he turned on a documentary to watch as a young woman berated the two of them. She hated Adams and Beckham, she said, but watched and read everything she could about them because of fascination about the details of their lives.

"I have never turned down a reasonable request for an autograph," Beckham wrote, but the sheer volume of such requests now made doing them unreasonable. He could not get through a meal at his favorite restaurants without an autograph line forming, an occurrence that caused him to eat more than one meal cold. He and Adams began to go to clubs where autograph seekers were not allowed, just so they could eat out without being hounded. When he had his long hair cut down to a buzz cut, the newspapers gave it more coverage than Manchester United's team performance.

British tabloid newspapers are notorious for their negative coverage of famous people, and the Beckhams became a favorite target. They used every trick in the book to catch the couple at their worst, even setting them up with intentionally embarrassing tricks. When Beckham and Adams left a restaurant one evening, two photographers were waiting. One of them got Beckham into a shouting match, while the other snapped pictures. The resulting photos showed Beckham yelling in anger, apparently out of control in public.

The idea of tormenting and hating someone because they are famous was a new concept for Beckham. To this day, Beckham remembers what it was like to be a young fan. He, too, had been an autograph seeker, which is why he did not like to turn down fans who wanted his signature. He certainly had not hated the famous footballers of his childhood. He sometimes wished he could reclaim some of the simpler pleasures of his youth, but he also knew there could be no going back.

seven

A Cold Farewell

As the pressures of fame mounted on Beckham, so did the pace of soccer battles for his team. Winning the Treble made a target of Manchester United, as the heavily crowned champions defended their titles.

Manchester United won the Premiership league cup again in 2000, but Beckham and his teammates ran into tougher competition in attempts to regain the FA Cup and Champions League. They did not win either of them. The press counted United's relatively lackluster season as a failure.

Manager Alex Ferguson tried to build a stronger defense to make United harder to beat in Europe, but it was not a success and the team finished the

2001-02 Premiership season in third place. They did not win another league title until the following (2002-2003) season. Ferguson continued to stew over Beckham's rise to superstardom, feeling his fame made Beckham consider himself above the rest of the squad. Beckham insisted nothing had changed, but relations between the two remained strained.

Controversy also overshadowed the national team. England's manager Glenn Hoddle got into troubles of his own when he made a careless remark about handicapped people. He said that the disabled were "paying for the sins of an earlier life," and was fired when the remarks stirred public outrage. England went into the European Championship with a new manager, Kevin Keegan.

Keegan had earned a reputation as a great footballer during his days as a player, but England stumbled badly under his leadership. In the drive to regain the Championship, England took leads against Romania and Portugal, but lost to both. The final straw for Keegan came in a World Cup qualifier against Germany in old Wembley Stadium in London. The historic stadium was slated to be torn down, and fans wanted to see the team send it off in style.

It was not to be. The Germans kept England from even mounting a threat, defending midfield so effectively that their British rivals finished scoreless. Keegan resigned after the game. He was succeeded by two interim managers, the second of whom was Peter Taylor.

Taylor gave Beckham one of the great honors of his career when he made him captain of the English team. Beckham took the call from Taylor at eight in the morning. "I was frozen to the spot by what I'd just heard: so excited, so proud, humbled by the thought of it," Beckham later wrote.

The next manager of the English team could have appointed a new captain. But when England named Sven-Goran Eriksson manager, Eriksson told Beckham he would stay in place as captain.

"You're a good enough player and a player others can look up to," Eriksson told him. "Anybody who doubts that, it's your job to prove them wrong."

Beckham got along well with Eriksson. He was even-tempered, at least by the standards of sports managers. He did not waste words with players, but he was less prone to berate them than Ferguson of United.

Beckham's time as captain of England was marked by good games, rather than championships. One of the team's greatest moments came in Munich against Germany, a longstanding archrival. They entered the match an underdog but defeated the German team on its own soil. Fans and players alike celebrated the victory as though they had won a major crown.

One of his personal bests came in a match against Greece in qualifying for the 2002 World Cup. This time, the Greeks were the underdogs. Greece scored just before half time, with England scoreless. During the break, Eriksson warned his team they would have to change the momentum to keep from being embarrassed by the Greeks. Beckham was fired up when England came back on. Teddy Sheringham scored to tie the match. The Greeks answered with another goal of their own. As time was running out, Sheringham won a free kick. As captain, Beckham could choose to take the kick himself. He booted the kick from twenty-five yards out. In classic Beckham style, the ball bent near the wall and sailed into the left side of the net.

England still needed some luck to qualify for the World Cup, with its fate depending on Finland's game against Germany. When the two teams tied, England qualified. Beckham's goal had launched his country's team into the next round of competition.

Beckham scores with a free kick to win the match between Greece and England in a World Cup Qualifier. *(Courtesy of Ross Kinnaird/Allsport)*

England did not go on to win the World Cup, but fans would always remember his great play. Beckham earned runner-up for World Player of the Year award.

Manchester United fortunes, on the other hand, were tanking. In the 2001-2002 season, the team won no trophies whatever. Their bitter rival Arsenal poured salt into the wound by winning the Premiership at United's Old Trafford home field. The press ruthlessly badgered manager Ferguson on the team's poor performance. They would regain their pride the next season, with an eighth league title in eleven years. Meanwhile, however, Ferguson continued to suspect that Beckham was not giving United his all.

Beckham said he was completely focused on the team, even while his personal life was becoming more complicated. Fans continued to taunt him, and even resorted to yelling nasty things about his son Brooklyn. With their family life under increasing scrutiny, Adams became pregnant with their second son. Adding to the stress, his parents divorced. Like many offspring who blame themselves for such breakups, Beckham wondered if he could have done anything to prevent it. His second son, Romeo, was born on September 1, 2002, just after the beginning of United's season.

Beckham's wife
Victoria holds their
second son, Romeo.
*(Courtesy of AP Images/
Owen Humphreys/PA)*

United would win the Premiership that season, but not before Ferguson and Beckham got into a dressing room quarrel that became legendary. Arsenal knocked United out of FA Cup contention with a win at Old Trafford. In the dressing room, Ferguson began berating Beckham, blaming him in large part for the loss. Beckham swore at the manager, a serious infraction for any player. A furious Ferguson kicked a shoe, sending it flying into Beckham's head, cutting a bloody gash above his eye.

The incident permanently damaged the relationship between the two men. Ferguson apologized, and even went out of his way to praise Beckham after later games. Although United ended its losing streak and went on to win the Premiership title, Beckham never felt the same about the coach who had helped start his career. Since Ferguson could decide who he wanted on the team, Beckham felt his days as a player for United were numbered.

His suspicions proved justified. Beckham and his family were vacationing at a desert resort in the United States when they saw the news on television. United had tentatively agreed on terms to sell him to the club in Barcelona, Spain.

"I was angry all right," Beckham recalled. "I didn't like the news, and how I'd found out about it, some

Beckham received this gash over the eye after Ferguson hit him with a shoe during a dressing room quarrel. *(Courtesy of Alex Livesey/Getty Images)*

time after the rest of the world, was humiliating."

He did not want to go to Barcelona, and eventually made a deal to go to another Spanish club, highly regarded Real Madrid. There was nothing he could do to change the situation with his home club. Like it or not, David Beckham had no future with Manchester United.

eight

Superstar in Madrid

Beckham shook off the insult of being sold to another club without his consent. There was a bright side, after all, in moving to Real Madrid. The Spanish club was one of the most successful clubs in football history. He put aside his anger and promised the management and fans of the new club that his loyalty now belonged to them.

Fan hysteria greeted the soccer superstar when he and Adams arrived in Madrid. Four police officers on motorcycles escorted his Audi 8 into the Spanish capital.

He had come for the routine hospital physical, but his presence created more fanfare than anyone might expect for a British prime minister. He stepped out of the car wearing jeans split at the knees, paired with a white shirt and jacket. Hundreds of fans shouted his name, as reporters yelled questions from behind a police barrier. Satellite news crews maneuvered to beam images of Beckham to their viewers. Even outpatients at the hospital were buttonholed by reporters beseeching them for anything they could see or overhear about Real Madrid's new star.

The club's medical examiner pronounced Beckham "fit as a bull." After the physical, he kicked the ball around with Brooklyn for a while at the club's Santiago Bernabeu stadium. Then he signed the contract and expressed gratitude to his new team.

"I've not dreamed about playing for many soccer clubs," he said. "There's not a player anywhere, though, who hasn't dreamt of playing for Real Madrid."

He spent three months living in an expensive hotel, one that hosted famous rock stars and actors. The only problem was that the hotel only had front and back entrances, so he and his bodyguards were forced to fight news crews and opportunistic photographers every time he came or went. He finally rented a huge estate about fifteen miles northwest of the city, complete with pool, tennis courts, and

Beckham takes the field in 2003 as a member of Real Madrid's soccer team. (*Courtesy of AP Images/Paul White*)

almost three acres of wooded grounds as a buffer between the Beckhams and the press.

The 2003-2004 season started well for his new team. Real Madrid soon took the top spot of the Spanish League. Beckham earned a reputation as a tough, disciplined player who contributed well, whether he scored or not. He earned acclaim when he played a major role in beating Barcelona. He helped score a key goal when he fired a well-aimed pass to Zinedine Zidane, who propelled the ball to Roberto Carlos. Carlos then kicked it past the Barcelona goalkeeper. The resulting victory was Madrid's first at Barcelona in twenty years.

But Real Madrid's season did not match expectations. The club had its eye set on three major titles: the Spanish Cup, the Champions League, and the Spanish League.

They made it to the finals of the Spanish Cup, only to fall to Zaragoza. Monaco bounced them out of the Champions League quarterfinals. They squandered their early lead in the Spanish League, and fell to a disappointing third-place finish. The fans did not blame Beckham, instead putting the burden for the losses on management.

Beckham kept his link to his home country by continuing to serve as the captain of England's national team. There, too, his fortunes were mixed. In the first round of the 2004 European Championship in Portugal, England fell to France. Coincidently, the winning goal came from Madrid teammate Zidane. After the early stumble, England bested Switzerland and Croatia to advance to the quarterfinal.

England played host Portugal and jumped to an early lead. But an injury turned the game in Portugal's favor when Wayne Rooney, a talented eighteen-year-old, had to be sidelined because of an injured foot. Portugal scored and sent the game into overtime, and went on to win the match. Beckham botched a penalty kick in the extra period, which made the loss all the worse for him.

Beckham did not see much team glory over the next two seasons. Real Madrid hit one of the more troubled periods in its fabled history in the 2004-2005 season. The team chased a strong Barcelona squad in the Spanish League, only to finish in second place. Valladolid knocked Madrid out of the Spanish Cup. Juventus tumbled them in the Champions League. The team took a beating in the press. Poor play cost two coaches their jobs.

The admiration of football fans burned bright for Beckham, even while the team went into free

Beckham reacts after missing a penalty kick against Portugal during the 2004 European Nations Championship quarterfinal match. *(Courtesy of Lluis Gene/AFP/Getty Images)*

fall. He earned points for being available to sign autographs for fans. As for the media, it behaved much as it had in England. Photographers and reporters had a passion for "Posh and Becks," much of it fueled by negativity. Adams spent little time in Madrid. Beckham chalked it up to her career demands, but news accounts read differently. They accused her of disliking the city, hating it for its lack of glamour, even reportedly saying it smelled bad.

The worst of it came when several women claimed to be Beckham's secret lovers. Adams apparently did not believe the reports, for she made a point of appearing with Beckham, arm in arm, after the first of the rumors surfaced. There was little she could do without getting criticism, however. Even when she made a show of affection, some writers accused the couple of staying together merely for the sake of keeping their "brand name" intact, so they could make more money than either would alone.

In August of 2004, the couple tilted the coverage in their favor when they announced the upcoming birth of their third son. Significantly, they pointed out that they planned for Adams to give birth in Madrid. Cruz David Beckham was born in February of 2005.

Unfortunately, the football did not get much better in the 2005-2006 season. Barcelona again beat them for the league. England's Arsenal knocked them out of the Champions League. The final blow came from Zaragoza, which downed them in the semifinals of

Beckham's body art

David's father Ted Beckham had tattoos when the boy was growing up, so the style never seemed strange to him. David has numerous tattoos and has admitted they can be something of an addiction.

His most prized body art consists of tributes to his family. David wears tattoos of his sons Brooklyn, Romeo, and Cruz, on his back, with their names, birth dates, and a guardian angel for each.

Three angels, or cherubs, are tattooed on his bicep, again representing his children. He has said he feels the tattoos make him feel closer to his children as he travels for matches. He has his wife Victoria's name tattooed in Hindi, the language of northern India. He also has the number seven, his team number at Manchester United.

His various religious tattoos have sometimes caused controversy. He has a guardian angel on his back and one resembling a painting of an angel by the artist Michelangelo on his right arm. When he got a four-by-six-inch winged cross done on the back of his neck, several London newspapers ran stories questioning whether they were appropriate. One writer wrote that the numerous body illustrations made him look like a member of the Hell's Angels, a violent biker gang.

Victoria Beckham wears body art of her own. She has five stars on her neck, and David's initials inked on her arm. Tattoo artist Louis Molloy has worked on both of the Beckhams' bodies.

the Spanish Cup. The fallout forced Real president Florentino Pèrez out of his job.

England was faring little better in its attempt to snag a World Cup. In a rematch of the game two years earlier, England faced Portugal in 2006. Beckham made good plays, but the end result was the same, as the English went down in defeat. After the defeat, Beckham decided it was time for him to step down as captain. At the same time, sports writers were questioning his contribution to the team, simply

Beckham displays some of his many tattoos. *(Courtesy of AP Images/Mark Baker)*

because everyone had expected better when Real Madrid signed a superstar.

Madrid's love affair with Beckham was coming to an end. Frustrated by bad press and bad football, Beckham began to feel his career in Spain had run its course.

nine

Beckham in America

Beckham's contract with Real Madrid came up for extension in 2007. He turned it down and soon announced a dramatic change of course. He would sign with the Los Angeles Galaxy, to play in U.S. Major League Soccer (MLS).

It would have been a surprise for any major European player, much less David Beckham, to go to the United States. Old-school fans in England are quite dismissive of the sport as played in the states, and consider it a dumping ground for the worst players. On the other hand, Beckham said he considered the move quite natural. He had already established a training camp called the David Beckham Academy near Los Angeles.

But the sum he was paid for the move got more notice than the decision to play in America. He would earn a breathtaking $250 million over five years. His salary would set a record for the highest in team sports history. Beckham insisted he did not go for the money. He and Adams already had plenty. Instead, Beckham called his signing with Galaxy an effort to establish a foothold for soccer in a country which traditionally regarded it as a minor sport.

"There are so many great sports in America," he said. "There are so many kids that play baseball, American football, basketball. But soccer is huge all around the world apart from America, so that's where I want to make a difference with the kids."

MLS officials also hoped for a boost from the world's most famous living player. MLS commissioner Don Garber called him, "a global sports icon who will transcend the sport of soccer in America."

The deal immediately paid dividends for Galaxy and the MSL. The morning after it was announced, the team sold a thousand season tickets.

His pending arrival excited some of his teammates as much as his fans. New draft pick Robbie Findley gushed about the opportunity to play with one of his idols.

Beckham's presence on the L.A. team has boosted ticket sales and excited U.S. soccer fans. *(Courtesy of AP Images/Nick Ut)*

"I've been looking up to him since I was a little kid," Findley said. "He's been one of the best players in the world. I've idolized him and now to get a chance to play with him. It will certainly help me learn the game, and hopefully it will raise the level of the league."

Soccer enthusiasts in his home country complained about Beckham's selling out. English soccer fans pass the sport from one generation to the next. In the U.S., on the other hand, many of his brand new fans know next to nothing about soccer. The only thing they knew was Beckham, the player famed for fame itself, adding charisma and good looks to his skill with the ball.

A move to Los Angeles made sense for both halves of the Posh and Becks phenomenon. The city is the entertainment capital of the world. Adams would be close to her music industry contacts. Hollywood actors and other celebrities watched Beckham's first American season with newfound interest. Los Angeles was also a natural for filming commercials for his sponsors, including adidas and Pepsi.

Real Madrid sports writers predicted he would flop. His first season showed little to prove them wrong. He suffered injuries to his tendons that sidelined him for much of the season. He made only two starts in nineteen league games.

One sports writer dismissed Beckham's first season as a failure but added that his fame was so great, it hardly mattered. Galaxy would still draw crowds with his name on its roster, and fans would remain devoted even if he performed poorly. "Beckham was

Beckham playing for the Los Angeles Galaxy team in 2007 *(Courtesy of AP Images/ Kevork Djansezian)* never going to sell soccer by playing the game," he wrote. "He was here to lend it glamour, to attract coverage and to serve as its spokesmodel."

It is not likely Beckham found comfort in such an easy excuse for poor play. He gained everything worth having by doing almost everything worth doing with a soccer ball. He has said he remembers much of his life by his best moments on the field, such as gaining redemption for his World Cup '98 fiasco by helping Manchester United win the Treble. The memory of his midfield goal against Wimbledon is another such frozen image, so clear in his memory it "feels like the ball is still up there."

He also remembers quite well the days when his reward for football amounted to a coin from his father and a pat on the back. Years before Beckham found fortune and celebrity, he was just a skinny kid working to keep the ball in the air with his feet. As a pro, he worked just as hard when fans met him with jeers as with praise. Beckham's fame is dazzling, but no one should underestimate his talent. How well he manages both will determine his legacy.

Timeline

1975 David Robert Joseph Beckham born on May 2 in London, England.

1991 Signs with Manchester United's youth team.

1992 Plays in first Manchester United game, against Brighton; team wins Football Association Youth Cup.

1993 Signs professional contract with Manchester United.

1996 Makes spectacular goal against Wimbledon, kicking the ball from midfield; performs as key player as United wins Premier League and FA Cup, called doing the "Double."

1997 Named Professional Footballers' Association Young Player of the Year; meets Victoria Adams, pop music star with the Spice Girls.

1998
Received red card in England's World Cup match against Argentina, for foul against Diego Simeone; resulting ejection from game leaves England short-handed; faces national scorn from fans and media after national team goes on to lose match; first son, Brooklyn, born on March 4.

1999
Turns in one of strongest season performances of career, helping United win the "Treble," with victories in Premier League, FA Cup, and Champions League; earns runner-up in World Player of the Year award; marries Adams.

2001
Named captain of England's national team by coach Sven-Goran Eriksson; kicks in 25-yard free kick to tie England with Greece, and clinches a place in World Cup competition; named runner-up for World Player of the Year.

2002
Second son, Romeo, born on September 1; scores against archrival Argentina in World Cup to

send team to 1-0 victory, but England loses to Brazil in quarterfinals.

2003 Dressing room argument with United manager Alex Ferguson results in Ferguson accidentally kicking boot in Beckham's face, leaving cut over left eye; Manchester United announces plans to trade Beckham; signs with Real Madrid of Spain.

2004 Accused by several women of having extramarital affair; denies rumors, and he and Victoria are seen together in public photographs soon after.

2005 Opens two David Beckham Academies to teach soccer skills to young players; third son, Cruz, born on February 20.

2006 Beckham helps lead England to the quarterfinals of World Cup, scoring on a free kick to notch 1-0 victory against Ecuador; England loses quarterfinal match against Portugal; resigns as captain of England.

2007 Declines contract extension with Real Madrid; signs with Los Angeles Galaxy.

Sources

CHAPTER ONE: Footballs for Christmas

p. 16, "little mate," David Beckham, *Beckham: Both Feet on the Ground* (Great Britain: CollinsWillow, 2004), 16.

p. 19, "I was so excited . . . " Ibid, 9.

p. 21, "That was the longest . . ." Ibid, 15.

p. 23, "That killed me . . ." David Beckham, *David Beckham: My World* (United Kingdom: Hodder & Stoughton, 2000), 10.

p. 25, "That man over . . ." Beckham, *Beckham: Both Feet on the Ground*, 24.

CHAPTER TWO: Fledgling Footballer

p. 27, "He said you're . . . " Beckham, *Beckham: Both Feet on the Ground*, 24.

p. 28, "What are you . . ." Ibid, 44.

CHAPTER THREE: Winning with Kids

p. 34, "right flash sod," David Beckham, *David Beckham's Soccer Skills*, 18.

p. 36, "you can't win . . . " "Manchester United: The Sir Alex Era-Part One," *BBC News*, January 31, 2007, http://www.bbc.co.uk/dna/h2g2/ A18740513.

p. 41, "Every schoolboy's dream . . ." Beckham, *Beckham: Both Feet on the Ground*, 78.

CHAPTER FOUR: Bending the Long Shot

p. 46, "When my foot . . ." Beckham, *Beckham: Both Feet on the Ground*, 83.

CHAPTER FIVE: Disgrace and Redemption

p. 67, "Manchester United have . . . " "Manchester United: 1999 Treble Archive," http://www. manutdtreble.com/european_cup.htm.

p. 58, "I have apologized . . . " "Beckham says sorry," *BBC News*, July 1, 1998, http://news.bbc. co.uk/1/hi/sport/football/124372.stm.

p. 58, "David Beckham's sending . . . " Ibid.

p. 59, "TEN HEROIC LIONS . . . " David Beckham, *Beckham: Both Feet on the Ground*, 132.

CHAPTER SIX: Posh and Becks

p. 73, "I have never . . . " Beckham, *David Beckham's Soccer Skills*, 87.

CHAPTER SEVEN: A Cold Farewell

p. 76, "paying for the . . . " Associated Press, "Turbulent Ending: England soccer coach Hoddle fired," *CNNSI.com*, February, 2, 1999, http://sportsillustrated.cnn. com/soccer/world/news/1999/02/02/hoddle_fired.

p. 77, "I was frozen . . ." Beckham, *Beckham: Both Feet on the Ground*, 203.

p. 77, "You're a good . . . " Ibid, 206.

p. 82, 84, "I was angry . . . " Ibid, 346.

CHAPTER EIGHT: Superstar in Madrid

p. 86, "fit as a bull," Gerard Couzens, *Viva El Becks: An Intimate Portrait of the World's Favourite Football Star* (London: Blake Publishing, 2005), 6.

p. 86, "I've not dreamed . . . " Beckham, *Beckham: Both Feet on the Ground*, 361.

CHAPTER NINE: Beckham in America

p. 96, "There are so . . . " Beth Harris, "David Beckham to Play for L.A. Galaxy," Associated Press, *washingtonpost.com*, January 11, 2007, http://www.washingtonpost.com/wp-dyn/content/article/2007/01/11/AR2007011102221.html.

p. 96, "a global sports . . . " Ibid.

p. 97, "I've been looking . . . " "Beckham joining MLS has draft picks excited," *USATODAY. com*, October 12, 2007, http://www.usatoday. com/printedition/sports/20070115/c12_soccer15. art.htm.

p. 98, 100, "Beckham was never . . . " Cathal Kelly,

"Beckham brand purrs on and on," *theStar.com*,
October 25, 2007, http://www.thestar.
com/Sports/article/270316.

p. 100, "feels like the . . . " Beckham, *Beckham:
Both Feet on the Ground*, 83.

Bibliography

Beckham, David. *Beckham: Both Feet on the Ground*. With Tom Watt. Great Britain: CollinsWillow, 2004.

Beckham, David. *David Beckham: My World*. United Kingdom: Hodder & Stoughton, 2000.

Beckham, David. *David Beckham's Soccer Skills*. New York: Collins, 2006.

Blackburn, Victoria. *David Beckham: The Great Betrayal*. London: Blake Publishing, 2003.

Couzens, Gerard. *Viva El Becks: An Intimate Portrait of the World's Favourite Football Star*. London: Blake Publishing, 2005.

Harrison, Paul. *David Beckham*. Chicago: Raintree, 2006.

Watson, Galadriel. *Remarkable People: David Beckham*. New York: Weigl Publishers, 2008.

Web sites

http://www.davidbeckham.com
Beckham's official Web site includes a blog, news articles, lifestyle photos, and more.

http://topics.nytimes.com/top/reference/timestopics/people/b/david_beckham/index.html?s=newest&
The *New York Times* features page after page of news about Beckham, dating back to 1998, including commentary and archival articles.

http://www.thedavidbeckhamacademy.com
The official Web site of the David Beckham academy.

Index